P9-BZA-246

Exploring the Galaxy
Mars

by Thomas K. Adamson

Consulting Editor: Gail Saunders-Smith, Ph.D.

Consultant: James Gerard
Aerospace Education Specialist, NASA
Kennedy Space Center, Florida

Capstone
press

Mankato, Minnesota

Pebble Plus is published by Capstone Press
151 Good Counsel Drive, P.O. Box 669, Mankato, Minnesota 56002
http://www.capstone-press.com

1 2 3 4 5 6 08 07 06 05 04 03

Library of Congress Cataloging-in-Publication Data
Adamson, Thomas K., 1970–
    Mars/by Thomas K. Adamson.
    p. cm.—(Pebble Plus: exploring the galaxy)
    Summary: Simple text and photographs describe the planet Mars.
    Includes bibliographical references and index.
    ISBN 0-7368-2113-9 (hardcover)
    1. Mars (Planet)—Juvenile literature. [1. Mars (Planet)] I. Title. II. Series.
QB641 .A33 2004
523.43—dc21   2002155605

Editorial Credits
Mari C. Schuh, editor; Kia Adams, designer; Alta Schaffer, photo researcher; Eric Kudalis, product planning editor

Photo Credits
Digital Vision, 5 (Venus), 19, 20–21
NASA, 4 (Pluto), 6–7, 8–9, 17; JPL, 5 (Jupiter), JPL/Caltech, 5 (Uranus), JPL/Malin Space Science Systems, 15
PhotoDisc Inc., cover, 4 (Neptune), 5 (Earth, Sun, Mars, Mercury, Saturn), 11 (both); PhotoDisc Imaging, 1; Stock Trek, 12–13

OCT _2003

Note to Parents and Teachers

The Exploring the Galaxy series supports national science standards related to earth science. This book describes and illustrates the planet Mars. The photographs support early readers in understanding the text. The repetition of words and phrases helps early readers learn new words. This book also introduces early readers to subject-specific vocabulary words, which are defined in the Glossary section. Early readers may need assistance to read some words and to use the Table of Contents, Glossary, Read More, Internet Sites, and Index/Word List sections of the book.

Word Count: 144
Early-Intervention Level: 15

Table of Contents

Mars

Mars is the fourth planet
from the Sun. Mars is called
the red planet.

The Solar System

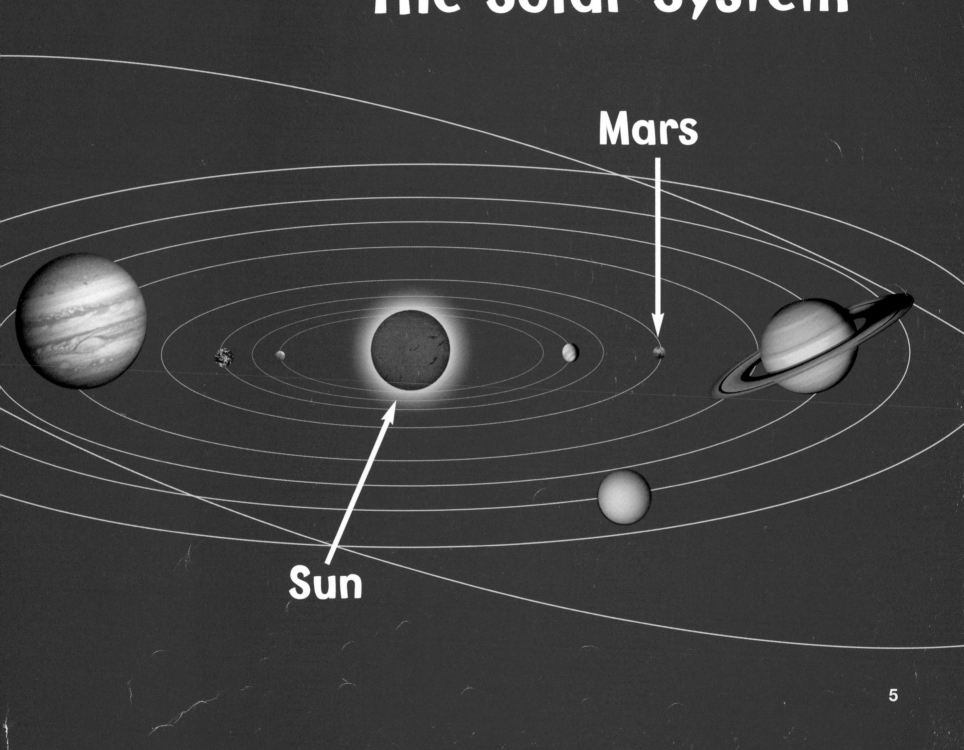

Mars

Sun

Surface of Mars

The red-brown surface of Mars is like a desert. Rocks cover the dry, dusty land on Mars.

Mars has deep canyons
and huge volcanoes.
Mars has ice at its poles.

9

Size of Mars

Mars is smaller than Earth.

Earth is about twice as wide

as Mars.

Earth

Mars

11

Air and Weather

The air on Mars is thin
and cold. People could not
breathe the air.

Dust storms happen often
on Mars. They can cover
the whole planet.

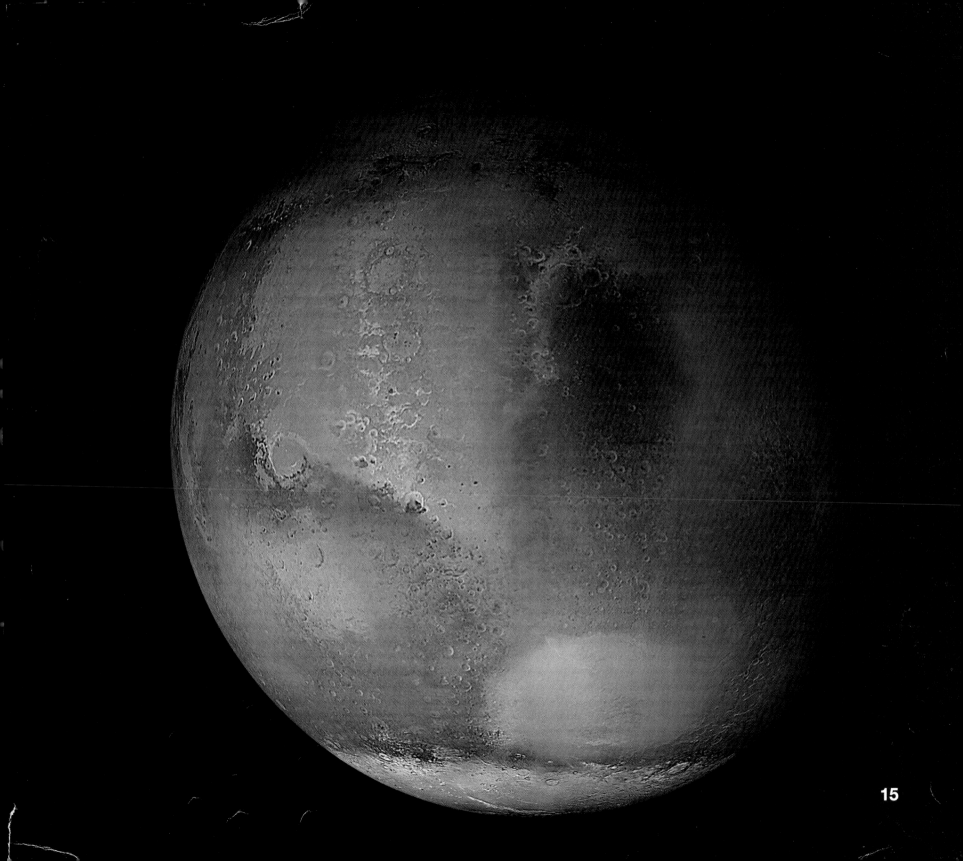

Exploring Mars

A trip to Mars from Earth
takes about six months. More
spacecraft have explored
Mars than any other planet.

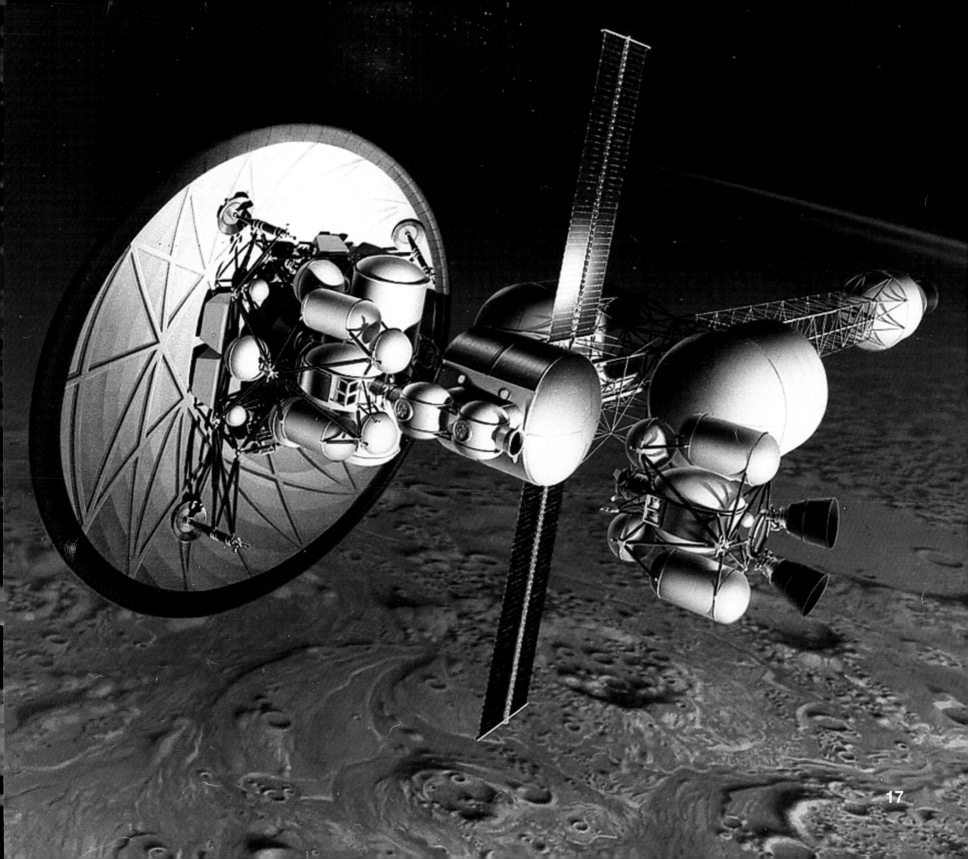

Scientists used a rover
to study rocks and dirt on
Mars. Scientists controlled
the rover from Earth.

Someday people might live
on Mars. They would have to
wear space suits. They would
need to build shelters that
hold air they can breathe.

Glossary

canyon—a long, deep valley with steep sides

crater—a large bowl-shaped hole in the ground

desert—a very dry area of land; deserts are sandy and rocky.

planet—a large object that moves around the Sun; Mars is the fourth planet from the Sun.

pole—the top or bottom part of a planet

rover—a small vehicle that people can move by using remote control; a rover called Sojourner explored Mars.

spacecraft—a vehicle used to travel in space; spacecraft that have traveled to Mars have not included people.

Sun—the star that the planets move around; the Sun provides light and heat for the planets.

volcano—a mountain with vents; melted rock oozes out of the vents; volcanoes on Mars are no longer active.

Read More

Carson, Mary Kay. *Mars.* Science Links. Philadelphia: Chelsea Clubhouse Books, 2003.

Goss, Tim. *Mars.* The Universe. Chicago: Heinemann Library, 2002.

Kerrod, Robin. *Mars.* Planet Library. Minneapolis: Lerner Publications, 2000.

Margaret, Amy. *Mars.* The Library of Planets. New York: PowerKids Press, 2001.

Internet Sites

Do you want to find out more about Mars and the solar system? Let FactHound, our fact-finding hound dog, do the research for you.

Here's how:

1) Visit *http://www.facthound.com*

2) Type in the **Book ID** number: **0736821139**

3) Click on **FETCH IT**.

FactHound will fetch Internet sites picked by our editors just for you!

Index/Word List